HOW THEY
LIVED

A SOLDIER IN WELLINGTON'S ARMY

FIONA SOMERSET FRY

Illustrated by
Mark Bergin

HOW THEY LIVED

Edited by Amanda Earl

First published in 1987 by
Wayland (Publishers) Limited
61 Western Road, Hove
East Sussex BN3 1JD, England

British Library Cataloguing in Publication Data
Somerset Fry, Fiona
A soldier in Wellington's army. – (How they lived/Wayland)
1. Peninsular War – Juvenile literature
I. Title II. Bergin, Mark III. Series
940.2′7 DC231

ISBN 0 85078 801 3

Phototypset by Kalligraphics Limited, Redhill, Surrey
Printed and bound in Belgium by Casterman S.A.

CONTENTS

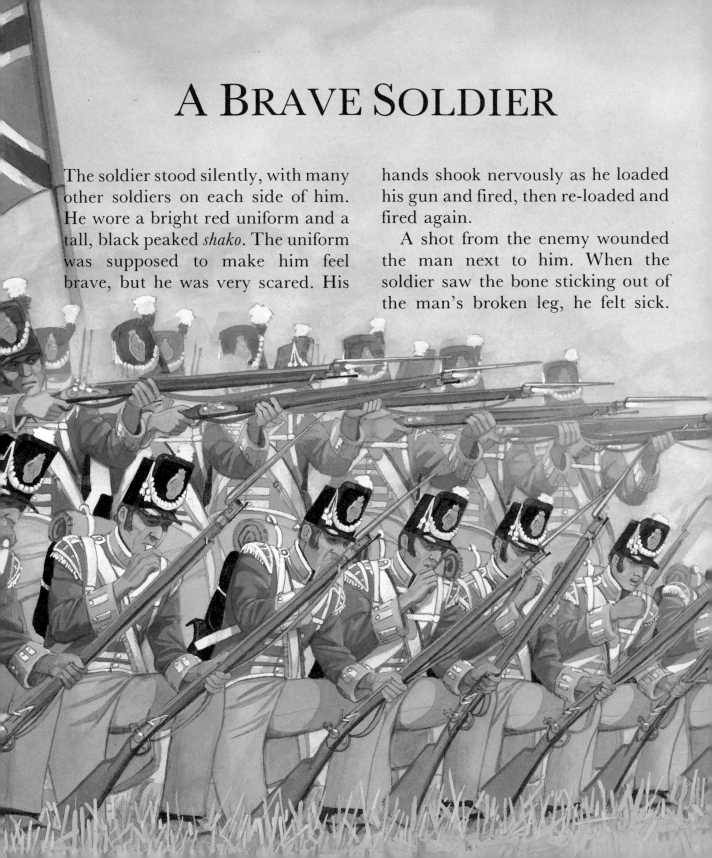

A BRAVE SOLDIER

The soldier stood silently, with many other soldiers on each side of him. He wore a bright red uniform and a tall, black peaked *shako*. The uniform was supposed to make him feel brave, but he was very scared. His hands shook nervously as he loaded his gun and fired, then re-loaded and fired again.

A shot from the enemy wounded the man next to him. When the soldier saw the bone sticking out of the man's broken leg, he felt sick.

Another shot killed his friend, who was standing close by. The soldier cried and tears streamed down his cheeks. An officer came galloping up on his horse shouting instructions, for the enemy was weakening and the line must go forward. The soldier, like his comrades, for a minute forgot his fear and ran excitedly ahead.

On a hill above the battlefield, the Duke of Wellington sat on his horse and watched. From this point, the two rows of infantry appeared as a thin red line. It was difficult to imagine from a distance that this army consisted of about 25,000 men, each figure looked so small.

Wellington was a very successful general, respected and trusted by his men. He commanded the British army which fought against Napoleon, the French Emperor who tried to conquer Europe. In the Peninsular War from 1808 to 1814, Wellington's army drove the French armies out of Portugal and Spain. Then in 1815, he completed Napoleon's defeat by winning the Battle of Waterloo.

A portrait of the Duke of Wellington in military uniform.

5

FOOT SOLDIERS

The infantry, or foot soldiers, were the backbone of Wellington's army. In battle they stood so close together their shoulders touched; each soldier was allowed only 56 cm (22 in) of space. They waited silently until the enemy infantry was about 92 m (100 yds) away, and then they opened fire with a deadly volley. When the enemy column reeled back, the British infantry charged, attacking enemy soldiers with bayonets, which were fixed to their gun barrels.

British foot soldiers (bottom left) form a 'square' to fend off the enemy's charge.

When enemy cavalry threatened to charge, the British infantry formed squares, consisting of two ranks of men standing ready to fire, and a third rank kneeling. Horses would not attempt to break through such an obstacle. After several cavalry attacks had failed, the ground would be so littered with the bodies of men and horses, dead and dying, that no further attacks were possible.

Most infantry regiments were armed with muskets, which fired small balls of lead or iron. After each volley, soldiers had to reload, biting off the end of a paper cartridge, pouring gunpowder down the barrel and ramming the ball in with an iron ramrod. A well-trained soldier could fire three shots a minute, but after ten minutes the barrel would be so clogged with gunpowder it would need cleaning.

Musket-fire was very inaccurate. If a soldier did hit a target more than 74 m (80 yds) away, it was due to luck rather than skill. Some infantry regiments used the rifle, which put a spin on the bullet and made it fly straight. But a rifle, with its grooved bore, was even more difficult to load than a musket.

CHARGING CAVALRY

The cavalry had to act quickly and bravely. Dragoons and hussars, as the soldiers who rode in the cavalry were called, fought on the edge of the battlefield. They aided the hard-pressed infantry, charged and disrupted the enemy cavalry and sometimes captured an enemy cannon. In victory, the cavalry pursued the fleeing enemy.

Just as the infantry stood shoulder to shoulder, the cavalry were trained to ride very close together. A mounted dragoon was allowed less

A recruitment poster of 1810 encouraging the dragoons to 'tread the paths of glory'.

THE OLD SAUCY
SEVENTH.
Or Queen's Own Regt. of
Lt. Dragoons.

COMMANDED BY THAT GALLANT AND WELL KNOWN HERO.

Lieut. General
HENRY LORD PAGET.

YOUNG Fellows whose hearts beat high to tread the paths of Glory, could not have a better opportunity than now offers. Come forward then, and Enrol yourselves in a Regiment that stands unrivalled, and where the kind treatment, the Men ever experienced is well known throughout the whole Kingdom.

Each Young Hero on being approved, will receive the largest Bounty allowed by Government.

A few smart Young Lads, will be taken at Sixteen Years of Age, 5 Feet 2 Inches, but they must be active, and well limbed. Apply to SERJEANT HOOPER, at

N. B. *This Regiment is mounted on Blood Horses, and being lately returned from SPAIN, and the Horses Young, the Men will not be allowed to HUNT during the next Season, more than once a week.*

A cavalryman of the Scots Greys.

than 1 m (approximately 1 yd) of space. In such close formation, a troop of dragoons had to be able to charge at full gallop, cutting and slashing at the enemy with their swords, or curved sabres.

A cavalry trooper was totally dependent on his horse, which had to be strong, bold and able to move quickly. Cavalry horses were generally black or brown in colour, but one famous regiment of dragoons used only grey horses. This regiment became known as the Scots Greys.

Cavalry, fighting on the edge of the battlefield, capture an enemy cannon.

9

Most battles started with gunfire from the heavy artillery positioned among the low hills which often overlooked a battlefield. The guns were swung round on wheels towards the enemy, and then fired in much the same way as a musket. Shot was rammed into the barrel and ignited with gunpowder, which was lit by a fuse. The gun recoiled so fiercely that it had to be aimed again after every shot. Nevertheless, a good team of gunners could fire a cannon twice in one minute.

Heavy guns fired round-shot — solid balls of iron weighing either 1½, 2½ or even 5½ kg. Fired at an advancing column, one round-shot could knock over and perhaps kill a

Left *Gunners move a cannon into position as the battle begins.*

Below *Soldiers re-aiming a cannon during a battle.*

row of 25 men. Soldiers would be able to see a round-shot coming due to its size, but they believed it was cowardly, rather than sensible, to duck! Guns sometimes fired hollow shells filled with gunpowder, which exploded on hitting the ground. Another type of ammunition was grape-shot which was made out of musket-balls (or scraps of iron) packed into a metal container. Grape-shot exploded in the air.

During a battle, horse artillery took lighter guns to the points where they were needed most. Each wheeled gun was hooked on to a gun carriage and dragged into position by four or six galloping horses. The horse artillery often helped the infantry when it was advancing. If you have ever seen horse artillery racing round the arena at the Royal Tournament, or any other military tattoo, you will know what it was like!

RECRUITMENT AND TRAINING

To find new recruits for Wellington's army, a sergeant would travel around to the small towns and villages, looking for suitable candidates. After gathering a large crowd around him, he would offer a king's shilling to any young man who would join Wellington's army, often with a bounty of £25 for those who enlisted. For some, this temptation was hard to resist, as £25 was a lot of money.

Before long, many young men had volunteered. Without having time to realize their fate, they were in the army!

On the first day, recruits had their hair cut and their colourful uniforms fitted. Training began very early the next morning, when soldiers went on parade. For up to five hours a day, new soldiers practised marching in step and obeying commands. They

When travelling around recruiting, sergeants would sometimes offer a bounty to young men who enlisted in Wellington's army.

also had to learn to carry their heavy equipment over long distances. Of one group of young recruits Wellington saw, he exclaimed, 'I don't know what effect those men will have on the enemy, but, by God, they terrify me!' He was referring to their lack of training and discipline.

Recruits to the cavalry started their training in riding schools. Most importantly, they had to learn to ride in formation and to charge – advancing from a walk to a trot and finally to full gallop. Gunners had to learn to work in teams, each man playing his part in the firing of a cannon.

Wellington's men performed very complicated movements in battle (similar to those seen today in the Trooping the Colour parade) – marching in columns, spreading out into lines and forming squares. Therefore, training was very important. Napoleon's forces hardly ever broke through the British infantry square during a battle. Hard training and constant practice helped to achieve this.

Recruits often found training very difficult at first. From early in the morning, soldiers practised marching and obeying their officer's commands.

13

AN OFFICER'S ROLE

In Wellington's day, as now, an officer had to lead his men – to direct them, encourage them, give them orders and see that they were obeyed. An officer had to be courageous, and yet he also had to be sensible enough not to put his men in unnecessary danger.

Wellington's officers were mostly young men from rich families. They paid large sums of money for the honour, as they saw it, of being a captain or a colonel. No one would pay to become an officer unless they really wanted a military life.

Officers had no training. They had all learned to ride and shoot at home, and when they joined their regiments, they were given an experienced sergeant to assist them. For the first few weeks at least, a young officer took his sergeant's advice.

Officers spent much of their time on horseback. They needed to move quickly from one column of men to another, to visit outposts and check possible troublespots. Officers on Wellington's staff acted as his messengers, galloping from place to place with his orders and bringing back reports of the battle's progress.

They enjoyed many privileges. They had extra rations, mules to carry their baggage and soldier-servants. A high-ranking officer, such as a general, might have two or three servants and a dozen pack animals to carry his personal belongings and furniture.

A portable camp bed used by officers in Wellington's army.

Officers were in charge of the soldiers under them, and it was important they received orders from their general quickly.

A Soldier's Uniform

Modern soldiers wear khaki uniforms so they can blend in with the countryside. In Wellington's day soldiers needed to be seen. If a soldier was spotted unexpectedly by the enemy, he was not likely to be killed or wounded because gunfire was so inaccurate. But it was important for a general to be able to recognize the regiments under his command and see their position. So soldiers of all nations wore very bright colours,

Above *An officer, like the man on the horse, wore a more elaborate and colourful uniform than an ordinary soldier (right).*

Left *A typical jacket worn by a dragoon in Wellington's army.*

16

Top *A shako, made from felt and leather. This one has two holes in the side, made by shell-fire.*

Bottom *A brass shoulder belt badge worn by the 58th Infantry Regiment.*

the French mostly blue, the Russians green, the Austrians white and the British mostly red.

The British usually wore red because it was the colour of the royal livery and the soldiers were servants of the king. However, dragoons and hussars often wore blue, and riflemen wore green. But their uniforms were not one colour all over. Their breeches were white, buff, blue, or grey, and their boots and tall peaked shakos were made of felt and black leather. Their collars, cuffs and lapels were blue, green, purple, yellow, or black, according to the regiment they belonged to, and they wore all kinds of coloured plumes, tassels, cords, badges and buttons. Officer's uniforms were particularly elaborate, with silk sashes and gold and silver trimmings. Even their sword hilts were decorated.

But Wellington's soldiers did not always look neat and clean. While on campaign their uniforms often wore out or got lost. They sometimes stripped the blue coats off dead French soldiers to replace their own, or had new trousers made from army blankets. On long marches their boots wore out and some soldiers ended up marching barefoot.

ON THE MARCH

The cavalry fanned out ahead of the army on the march, looking for signs of the enemy or an ambush. Then came the artillery, drawn by teams of horses. The infantry followed in columns, each man carrying his equipment on his back – a rolled-up blanket, a knapsack containing spare clothing, a ration of meat and bread (or biscuit), a water-bottle, a hatchet or a spade, a musket or rifle, a bayonet, a cartridge-pouch and 80 rounds of ammunition. Altogether, it weighed about 27 kg (60lb).

Before the march began, the regimental bugles roused the men an hour and a half before dawn. By the time it was light, the horses would be fed, watered and saddled, the pack-mules loaded, the bullocks hitched to the ammunition waggons and every man was ready to move off.

The first stop or halt, was half an hour later, when for five minutes the men could adjust their loads and eat a piece of hard, dry biscuit, while those who had fallen behind caught up. After that, the stops were every hour or so.

When the army was advancing, the regimental bands played and the men's spirits were high, even in the intense heat of the Spanish summer. When the army occasionally retreated, as they did in November, 1812, they had to march night and day, in snow or pouring rain, to escape the enemy. In this march many of Wellington's soldiers died from hunger and exhaustion.

Below *A Brown Bess musket, the type of gun used by Wellington's soldiers.*

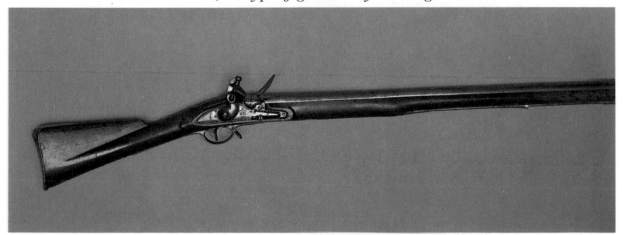

THE BAGGAGE TRAIN

Napoleon said that an army marches on its stomach – meaning that soldiers march and fight better if they are properly fed. Wellington also paid attention to this. When his army was on the march, it was followed by a long baggage train carrying

meat and flour, gin and rum for the soldiers, as well as hay for the horses and mules, spare blankets, boots, weapons and ammunition.

Each regiment of about a thousand men was allowed 13 pack-mules to carry its tents and stores.

When Wellington's army was on the move, it was followed by a long baggage train, carrying all its vital supplies – food, clothing, blankets, weapons and even furniture!

Besides that, its officers would have another 30 or 40 mules to carry their own tents, military chests of clothing and personal belongings, camp beds, tables and chairs, and luxuries such as tea and sugar.

Ammunition waggons, which carried gunpowder as well as shot, were kept well away from the rest of the baggage train. Gunpowder was highly dangerous. A spark from a camp fire could cause a terrible explosion.

A few soldiers from each regiment were allowed to take their wives on campaign. These women and their children walked or sometimes travelled on donkeys with the baggage train. They rejoined their husbands when the day's march was over, but soldiers never had a private tent with their families.

IN CAMP

If soldiers were lucky, they would end their march before nightfall in a village or small town, where they could stay in cottages and barns. More often they just pitched their tents in fields, or bivouacked, that is, made a camp without tents.

The chosen spot would be near a wood, so the soldiers could cut sticks for camp fires, and by a stream, where they could wash, fill their water-bottles and let the animals drink.

Sentries, posted as look-outs, would be changed every two hours throughout the night. The officers

Soldiers usually stopped for the night near a wood and made a camp. Food was then prepared on an open fire.

used their time at camp to make plans for the next day, while soldiers cooked food on the camp fires. They made a kind of oatmeal porridge called *stirabout*, and their meat ration was either boiled, or roasted on the points of their swords or bayonets over the fire. They talked, smoked, cleaned their weapons and drank their issue of gin or rum. If they had no tent, they often just fell asleep around the camp fire.

Camp life was enjoyable in fine weather, but everyone suffered in the wet and cold. Clothes were not waterproof in those days, and while a tent, or even the leaves of a tree, might keep off driving rain, men lying in the open soon became soaked to the skin.

Normally soldiers put their weapons in a pile and took off their

The type of field canteen used by Wellington's officers.

uniforms to sleep. But if the enemy was near and a sudden attack likely, they kept their rifles and muskets beside them and slept fully dressed.

Napoleon's soldiers, like Wellington's, suffered in bad weather. Here they are seen after spending a night in the cold on the morning of the Battle of Waterloo.

WINTER QUARTERS

Armies only fought in the summer. During the winter they returned to base or made a camp wherever they happened to be. Wellington's army spent several winters in Portugal, near Lisbon, and another in the Pyrenees mountains.

The army could relax in Portugal. Wellington and other officers had

In winter quarters, soldiers relaxed with the local girls.

their own packs of foxhounds 'there and were able to hunt every other day; the exercise kept both horse and rider fit. There was shooting and fishing as well, and a race meeting every Wednesday. Officers led a lively social life in winter quarters.

The ordinary soldiers had too little money for such lavish entertainment. They were paid about 1 shilling a day, only half the wage of a ploughman in England, and most of that went on food and the care of their uniforms. But soldiers did enjoy themselves sometimes. They made friends with the local Portuguese girls, went for walks in the town and

Wellington and his army arrive in a Spanish town during a campaign.

listened to music played by the regimental bands.

The mountains of the Pyrenees were far less pleasant than sunny Portugal. When Wellington's army spent the winter in the Pyrenees it rained and snowed, torrents of water flooded into the valleys, and the army suffered terribly. The wooden huts of the temporary encampment could not keep out the cold or the damp. Yet everyone was cheerful — for the army had chased the French out of Spain and back into France.

DISCIPLINE
AND PUNISHMENT

Discipline plays an essential part in any army. A battle cannot be won unless the commanding officer's orders are carried out by the people

under him. Yet, discipline in Wellington's army was dreadfully harsh.

The punishment of officers was light. They were either reprimanded, removed from their duties or sent out of the army for misbehaviour. A disgraced officer had his sword broken. But for the ordinary soldiers, the infantry, the cavalry and the gunners, punishment was severe. If a soldier struck an officer, tried to desert to the enemy, or robbed one of the local people with violence, he would be shot. If he was caught thieving or looting, he was sentenced to 300, 500 or 700 lashes with a cat-o'-nine-tails. For a trivial offence, such as making a mistake on parade, a soldier would receive 25 to a 100 lashes.

Punishments were always carried out in public. The whole regiment would be lined up for a flogging. The prisoner would be tied up, and each stroke of the lash was accompanied by the slow beat of a drum. A surgeon was always there to see the victim was not too badly injured. Nevertheless most men spent several weeks in hospital to recover after a flogging, and some died.

But too much punishment of the soldiers often caused problems. A good and willing soldier, who was severely beaten for a slight mistake, would lose heart and, with it, his will to fight.

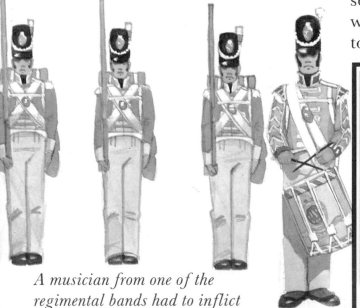

A musician from one of the regimental bands had to inflict punishment, but he did not like his task.

An army deserter is captured.

TREATING THE WOUNDED

Before a battle, army surgeons set up their medical posts in nearby cottages and farm buildings. Each one had an operating table, and another table beside it for bowls of water and the surgeon's equipment.

There were no anaesthetics, as they had not been invented. A wounded man was given wine, or rum and water. Then the surgeon probed the open wound with his fingers for musket balls. Sometimes he found pieces of cloth, leather and scraps of metal as well. Chest and

A surgeon treats injured soldiers at a makeshift medical post.

stomach wounds were stitched up with needle and thread, flesh wounds were bandaged and broken bones were set with wooden splints. But a badly damaged arm or leg had to be amputated, usually to safeguard against gangrene. The patient was held down on the operating table, while the surgeon sawed quickly through the bone.

Today, we cannot understand how a man could endure the pain of an amputation without an anaesthetic.

Wives and soldiers return to the battlefield to help the wounded.

A set of surgeon's instruments from the Peninsular War. The saws were used when soldiers had to have a limb amputated.

But in those days, people accepted pain – everyone suffered it at some time or other, and the surgeons in Wellington's army had a very good record. Nine out of ten of those soldiers who had a limb amputated recovered.

Wounded men left on the battlefield were less fortunate. No one helped them. After the battle, looters came to look for jewellery, watches, money, gold from uniforms and false teeth to steal. They even killed some of the wounded. A day or two later, when the dead were taken for burial, the wounded who still survived were carried in carts to the nearest town.

WHEN THE WAR WAS OVER

In 1815, Napoleon was finally defeated by Wellington's army at the Battle of Waterloo. Soldiers had always dreamed of peace, of winning their battles, and now the more fortunate ones could return home to their families. Yet, it is important to remember that over a quarter of the soldiers in Wellington's army were killed, and many others came home badly injured.

Some soldiers received a small pension, while others were left to scrape a living as best they could. The lucky ones were looked after in homes specially built for old soldiers.

All of them had tales to tell for the rest of their lives. They were heroes, who had shared adventure, hardship and glory, such as those at home had never known. They were given no medals, but their courage had been proved in the most terrible of all human activities – war.

A soldier returns home to his family at last to tell tales of what it was like to have been a soldier in Wellington's army.

GLOSSARY

Ambush   A hidden group of people waiting to make a surprise attack.

Amputate   To cut off a badly injured limb.

Anaesthetic   A drug, which puts a person to sleep during surgery.

Artillery   Heavy guns used for fighting on land, i.e. cannon.

Bayonet   A steel dagger which can be fixed to the gun barrel of a rifle or musket.

Bounty   Money sometimes given to new recruits on enlistment in the army.

Cat-o'-nine-tails   A whip with nine thin cords, used for flogging.

Courageous   Brave and fearless.

Discipline   Strict training in order to improve one's behaviour.

Enlist   To join the army.

Field Canteen   A selection of plates and eating utensils, used by officers in camp.

Gangrene   A very serious complaint, caused by a lack of blood circulation to a part of the body, resulting in poisoning.

Gunners   Soldiers in charge of heavy artillery.

Hard-pressed   To be under severe military attack.

Hilt   The handle of a sword or dagger.

King's shilling   Until 1879, a shilling was given to new recruits to the British army.

Looting   Stealing other people's belongings during a crisis or war.

Pack animals   Animals, usually horses and mules, which carry goods.

Recoil   The force or 'kick-back' of a gun after firing.

Recruit   A newly-enlisted member of the army.

Royal livery   The uniform worn by officials and servants of the king's court.

Shako   A cylindrical-shaped military hat with a peak.

Shilling   A silver-coloured coin worth approximately 5p today. In Wellington's day it was worth a good deal more.

Volley   The firing of many guns at the same time.

MORE BOOKS TO READ

Michael Barthorp, *British Infantry Uniforms since 1660* (Blandford, 1982)

Alan Blackwood, *Napoleon* (Wayland, 1986)

Gerald Allan Embleton, *Warfare in History* (Wayland, 1984)

Kenneth Ullyatt, *Hussars of the Napoleonic Wars* (Macdonald, 1981)

Martin Windrow, *The British Redcoat of the Napoleonic Wars* (Franklin Watts, 1985)

Martin Windrow, *The Foot Soldier* (Oxford University Press, 1983)

INDEX

Picture acknowledgements

The Bridgeman Art Library 19; Mary Evans Picture Library 11, 25, 29 (top); National Army Museum 8 (both), 14, 16 (left), 17 (both), 23 (top), 27, 29 (left); Sheffield City Art Gallery 23 (bottom); TOPHAM 5; Victoria and Albert Museum 6–7.

32